GW00838864

ANTONYMS & OTHERS

Other works by the author include

Poem About Music, 1974
Blood Flow, 1975
Fear and Misadventure & Mud Settles, 1977
North, North, I Said, No, Wait a Minute, South,
Oh, I Don't Know (148 Political Poems), 1985
The Résting Bĕll [Collected Poems], 1987
Carp and Rubato, 1995
Anti-Beauty, 1995
Lisa Lisa, 2000
Etiquette in the City, 2001
Miscanthus:
Selected and New Poems [with Prose], 2004
Citations followed on, 2010

Anthony Barnett

Antonyms & Others

Antonyms

Patricia of the Waters

Seventeen Poems of Defencelessness

Icing and Noticing

And When I Sleep I Do Not Weep

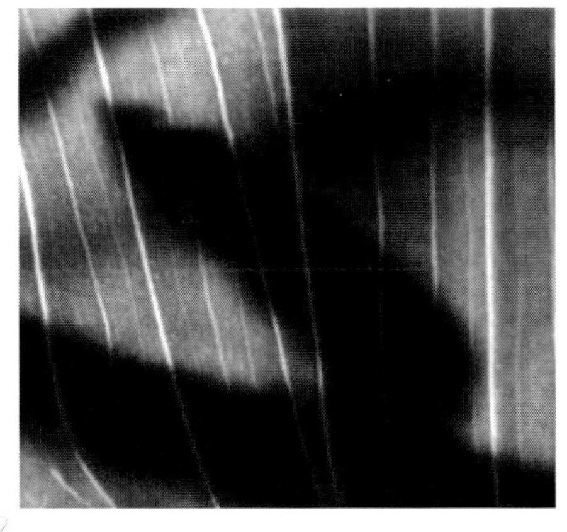

A·B

Antonyms I–VI first appeared in 2009–2011
in The Use of English under the editorship
of Ian Brinton for the English Association
There are amendments & additions to them here
17 Poems of Defencelessness were written 2010
Some first appeared in 2011 in
Tears in the Fence & Notre Dame Review
The Publisher, also an Antonym, was written 2010
It & three prosays appear here for the first time
Icing and Noticing was written 2010–2011
Patricia of the Waters & And When I Sleep I Do Not Weep
were begun circa 2000–2001 & slightly revised in 2011
A few other pieces from unfinished And When I Sleep are
printed in Miscanthus: Selected & New Poems (2005)

The reworked appropriated image shows the shadow
of a leaf cutter ant carrying a leaf - & a bee

Allardyce Book
imprint of
Allardyce, Barnett, Publishers
14 Mount Street · Lewes · East Sussex BN7 1HL UK
www.abar.net

Distributed in USA by
SPD Inc., Berkeley CA
www.spdbooks.org

Typset in Adobe Garamond by AB©omposer with 1st
epigraph in Song & imprint device in Centaur MT
Printed by CPI ARowe EUK

CIP records for this book are available from
The British Library and The Library of Congress

ISBN 978-0-907954-40-8

正言若反

一

gold begets black

Antonyms

On a Translation

It is so disappointing when a rare opportunity is lost. I speak of *The Selected Poetry and Prose of Andrea Zanzotto* (University of Chicago Press, 2007). Though magnificent when, rarely, one is grasped, for example, Timothy Billings and Christopher Bush's two-volume Victor Segalen *Stèles* (Wesleyan University Press, 2007).

Ten years ago, in "Between the Recent Past and the Distant Present", Zanzotto, arguing his case, which does not immediately concern me here, commended the award of the Nobel Prize for Literature to his countryman Dario Fo. That was generous coming from the one poet who long may have deserved the prize before any other, presupposing socio-ethical acceptance of such ranking and prizing.

The trouble with editor-translator Patrick Barron's *Selected Zanzotto* is that it is a hodgepodge (or hotchpotch in Brit. usage) of new translations mixed up with previously published translations, without, as far as I can see, required revision, from a variety of sources, some good but others, such as *Selected Poetry of Andrea Zanzotto* (Princeton University Press, 1975), notably incompetent. Ruth Feldman and Brian Swann's versions therein suffered fourfold guilt: error (example: "German machine-guns" instead of "machine-guns Germans"); clumsiness through reductionist, explanatory, normalized translations (example of the first: "cold jokes" instead of "stone cold jokes" for "barzellette freddissime"; example of the second: "ill-hatched from a cocoon" instead of "badly ecloded" for "male sbozzolato", which Barron thinks fitting enough to keep for his own new version [why is perfect, perfectly formed, perfectly current, "eclode" not to be found in the current edition of the *OED*?]; example of the third: "—The woman teacher says so / Lewis and Alice say so." instead of "—Miss Teacher says so / Lewis and Alice says so." for "—La maestra lo dice / lo dice Lewis e Alice."); lack of imagination, or poetry (example, about the silkworm: "they go to the woods they moult / they rot they sleep like logs" instead of, for example, "they go to the shed go to shed / go to the dogs sleep like the dead" for "vanno al bosco vanno in muda / vanno in vacca dormono della quarta"). And the fourth? Failure to translate at all. Two examples: "The Elegy in Petèl". Why not "Elegy in Googoo"? (Beverly Allen in *Andrea Zanzotto: The Language of Beauty's Apprentice* [University of California Press, 1988] has a pretty ineffectual stab in "The Baby-Talk Elegy"); and "e 'vé paidi tut" accompanied by the translators' note "Veneto dialect for 'I had assimilated digested and expelled everything'." What's wrong with "took it in spat it out the lot"? That's my dialect. Then there is the unthought through: Barron's "Strange name, dandelion" for "taràssaco", one of several designations Zanzotto uses for the herb in the same poem, is not strange. "Cranky name, cankerwort" gets it.

As well as poetry, Zanzotto is the author of several collections of exemplary poetic and critical essays. A feature of the Chicago selection, welcomed because it is a first, is the inclusion of a number of these. But again, there is a caveat, this time probably to be laid at the door of publisher rather than editor: there are not enough of them and they are relegated to the back, as if an afterthought, in lip service to a body of beautiful writing deserving no less than its own dedicated volumes. There is, then, a good long way to go before the totality, or even a satisfactory portion, of the work of this commentator's Nobel candidate receives proper care and consideration from professional English-language interpreters.

NOTE

I draw here on an unpublished paper "Some Poems Encountered in Translating the Problems of Andrea Zanzotto and Other Anecdotes of Literary Translation" presented in The Dark Room at *The Cambridge Conference of Contemporary Poetry*, 13 April 1991. My few translations were published in *Poems by Zanzotto* (AB, 1993) with a few more as an appendix to my *Anti-Beauty* (AB, 1999), in two issues of the review *Tears in the Fence* (2010–2011) and in *World Literature Today* (2011). It would be remiss were I not to acknowledge that I too of course am guilty of infelicity (it appears, for example, that I have missed some, though not all, Dante references) but I grappled and in places I came out tops. As for dandelion, there are so many common or local English names from which to choose to try to match Zanzotto's.

The Serious Writer

Were a young would-be writer of serious intent to ask: from whom among authors of the last century may I first and most learn? my choice would be the Austrian essayist and novelist Robert Musil, no matter what the language, at least European, beyond even, of our author or our would-be.

When Musil (1880–1942) is read in English it is usually as the author of a turn-of-the-century novel of adolescent sadism surrounding a military academy, *The Confusions of Young Törless*, critically prescient of what would become the era of nazism and fascism, and his unfinished magnum opus *The Man Without Qualities*, an encyclopedic, in the word of one of its translators Burton Pike, novel of society, an empire, in free-fall. From the mesmerised protagonists' points of view this takes place in slow motion. There is also a volume of immaculate novellas, reissued as *Five Women* (previously *Tonka and Other Stories*), and a play *The Enthusiasts.* But for reason of wanting to draw attention to what I believe to be Musil's less considered non-fictional writings, I describe him here as essayist and novelist, not the other way round.

Since the 1980s such other works have been available in English in *Posthumous Papers of a Living Author* (Hygiene, CO, Eridanos, 1987; repr. New York, Archipelago, 2006), which, as the title declares, is not posthumous, *Precision and Soul: Essays and Addresses* (University of Chicago Press, 1990) and *Diaries, 1899–1941* (New York, Basic Books, 1999), along with new, alternative versions of the two novels. *Selected Writings* (New York, Continuum, 1986) includes alternatives of a few of the shorter pieces. Thus there is no longer excuse for ignoring the near totality of this essential author.

Doubtless it is unfashionable today to write the word "soul" though taken as it can be it remains nothing but relevant. In a 1922 essay "Helpless Europe" Musil writes of "an abiding miscommunication between the intellect and the soul. We do not have too much intellect and too little soul, but too little intellect in matters of the soul." Yet he is able to preface this "Digressive Journey" with "The author is more modest and less obliging than the title of this piece might lead one to infer. Indeed, I am convinced not only that what I say is wrong, but that what will be said against it will be wrong as well." Turning to his 1934 lecture "The Serious Writer in Our Time": "And because I am speaking about the serious writer and about today the beginning is easy, because I can confidently claim that we don't know what either one is." The lecture unfolds to show that while "we" may not know, Musil most certainly does.

Musil's insights, appreciations, critiques, are passionate and cucumber cool, pedagogic by accident and default. He shakes down the ramifications of psychology and morality and ethics and mores (or whatever else one can be comfortable with in calling and differentiating the like) while he tempers his stories with scepticism and comedy. An eloquent and robust prose appears to be well served by translators—though great novels are supposed to be capable of withstanding most anything, the reader who is not to be taken in making any necessary adjustments along the way—so that: should our serious young would-be need to read Musil in English, language will be no stumbling block.

Acerbic commentaries on cultural artifacts and personages, such as the penpusher and the paintspreader and the poet and the painter, prefigure his countryman Thomas Bernhard but where Bernhard's art requires him to be clear as mud, Musil is just clear. Musil, then, though radical in his fictional technique—Italo Svevo also comes to mind—is not an overt linguistic innovator in, for example, the Joycean sense; nor does he necessarily have to be upheld as the model of his time, and he is certainly not to be imitated—no one should be—but rather as a master and mentor of the theory and practice of the art and science of writing and critiquing. If the presumption that he does not figure high on most reading lists is not an injustice to the reader I hope I have offered some small, if inadequate, reasons why it might be a good idea if he did. For a start, my own thinking and writing would be better off were I myself to listen more often to my own advice. No or at least few illusions.

Musil has a short story "A Man Without Character" which, in the translation by Peter Wortsman, ends: "It was clear to me, if I may say so, that he would have liked to be himself again; but something held him back."

Words in Black and White

Anyone looking to support an argument for the stupidity or futility of cinema might be forgiven for thinking it is to be found in three vignettes by Osip Mandelstam and Joseph Roth but that is not proven. True, they do not devote enthusiastic attention to the subject elsewhere, unlike some other significant literary essayists of the period, for example, their compatriots Isaac Babel, who wrote screenplays based on his own and others' stories, and Robert Musil, who critically embraced the medium. Nevertheless, there is something to say about an uneasy relationship between literature and film, such as the way film can freeze, freeze frame, the viewer's imagination in a way that the reader's may not be. Nor do I think the examples I have chosen from the earlier days of the cinema are any the less valid for that.

In "I Write a Scenario" (circa late 1920s, unpublished in his lifetime), Mandelstam does pay ambiguous homage to a Russian master: "A magnificent frame in the style of Eisenstein immediately comes to mind [. . .]" Ambiguous because I do detect a note of irony. I also detect such a note in Roth's "The Cinema in the Arena" (*Frankfurter Zeitung*, 1925), his report of a screening in the open air, "no longer a church but a cinema", at Nîmes of *The Ten Commandments* "that great American film that has already been shown in Germany." "At a time when these commandments are not much obeyed," Roth writes, "that's already saying something."

To his quick chagrin, Mandelstam has been advised by an influential well-wisher, Shklovsky, who then does a disappearing act, leaving Mandelstam to his own devices, to write for the cinema: "I decided to try to write a scenario about the life of a fire brigade." "Then", "On the other hand", "Yes", "But, why", "What", "No", "Or maybe", "No, that's no good", "How about", "But", "All right". These are just some of Mandelstam's fits and starts to what he cannot finish. You have to read this hilarious piece in its brief entirety but until you have, unless you already have, Mandelstam finishes: "Film is not literature. One must think in frames. / Let the Fire Chief be on duty in the theater, while his friend treats his wife to pastries. / No, this is absurd. / My theme burned up in the creative process. My mind is blank. I've got to catch that Shklovsky."

Roth experiences a similar epiphany: "It was a good idea to put on a film in the old Roman arena. In such a cinema you come to comforting conclusions, as long as you look at the sky, rather than the screen." A few months later, in Marseilles, at the Cosmos, "A Cinema in the Harbour" (also *Frankfurter Zeitung*, 1925), there are ruckuses during the screening of a film entitled *Red Wolves*, among the children and among the adults too, among the latter because they do not approve of the tune being banged out on the accompanying piano. A father, after reassuring himself of his little ones' safety—they are seated either side of Roth—"turns to attend to whatever events are now in progress, be they on the screen or in some other part of the cinema." And Roth would like to turn the tables on the actors and the audience: "I like to imagine the robbers in the Abruzzi going to the cinema to see a film about the sea dogs of Marseilles." Roth has held on to his imagination.

There is, in fact, a most beautiful movie of Roth's prescient last, 1939, novella: *The Legend of the Holy Drinker* (1988). I remember it as beautiful, and I remember Roth's story, but I can hardly remember the film, because, I assume because, it is in colour—or is a small part of it in black and white? I would have to see it again.

Black and white movies are often those that I remember best, that I want to but do not have to see again. Two miraculous literary adaptations spring to mind. *Hunger* (1968) from the influential novel by Knut Hamsun. I do not think there has ever been a film more faithful to its turn-of-the-century original in its transfer to its new medium. *Mr Thank You* (1936) a gem of a full length feature cut—developed, I should say—from the tiniest of early tales by Kawabata about a chauffeur who thanks everyone he passes for making way for his bus on the narrow coastal roads between the provinces and the city. It is astounding how the passengers' lives are, yes, brought to life. I don't want to talk more about these films. I would just like you to see these examples of the unfrozen imagination—words in black and white—unless you already have.

NOTE

STORIES AND ESSAYS: Osip Mandelstam's "I Write a Scenario" is included in *The Complete Critical Prose and Letters*, trans. Harris (Ann Arbor, Ardis, 1979). Joseph Roth's "The Cinema in the Arena" and "A Cinema in the Harbor" are included in *Report from a Parisian Paradise: Essays from France, 1925–1939*, trans. Hofmann (New York, Norton, 2004), also as *The White Cities* (London, Granta, 2004). Isaac Babel's screenplays are included in *The Complete Works*, trans. Constantine (New York, Norton, 2002). Robert Musil's 1926 "Cinema or Theater", for example, is included in *Precision and Soul: Essays and Addresses*, trans. Pike and Luft (University of Chicago Press, 1990). Yet in his 1937 lecture "On Stupidity", ibid., Musil could still jibe: "or it might perchance be the vacuously general, like the transformation of critical judgment by business, since God, in that goodness of his that is so hard for us to understand, has also bestowed the language of mankind on the creators of sound movies." Roth's *The Legend of the Holy Drinker*, trans. Hofmann (London, Chatto & Windus, 1989). Translations of Knut Hamsun's *Hunger* are Egerton (London, Duckworth, 1921), Bly (London, Duckworth, 1974), Lyngstad (Edinburgh, Cannongate, 1996). They are all good in their ways but I would like to suggest my own alternative to their opening sentences: "It was during the time I wandered about and starved in Kristiania, that passing strange city no one leaves before it has marked him." Kawabata Yasunari's "Thank You" (1925) is included in *Palm-of-the-Hand Stories*, trans. Dunlop and Holman (New York, Farrar, Straus and Giroux, 1988). There are later editions of all these.

FILMS: In Nîmes Roth sees *The Ten Commandments* directed by Cecil B. DeMille (1923) and in Marseilles *Red Wolves*, an unidentified, seemingly Italian, movie. *The Legend of the Holy Drinker* is an Italian film with an international cast, directed by Ermanno Olmi (1988). *Hunger* is a Nordic co-production, directed by Henning Carlson (1968). *Mr Thank You* is directed by Shimizu Hiroshi, who also wrote the screenplay (1936). The Japanese DVD *Arigatō-san* includes English subtitles.

The Notebook of José Saramago

José Saramago is a wonderful, in more senses than one, Portuguese novelist who won the Nobel Prize for Literature in 1998. I say is but I should say was because he died in June 2010 just two months after *The Notebook* appeared in English and two months short of a year following its last entry. But I prefer to say is because I am reading a notebook, *The Notebook*, as relevant in the present and, I think, the future, as it is in the recent past. *The Notebook* collects a year's blog entries posted by Saramago between September 2008 and August 2009, the almost daily task proposed by his wife Pilar and administrated with the assistance of two colleagues.

Now might be a good time to explain how the column in front of you came about. I reviewed a book for *The Use of English*. A bit of a mistake because our editor proposed I write more reviews. No, I did not want to. More than half in jest I suggested I contribute a series of "Antonym" commentaries. I had long harboured thoughts of such a weekly or monthly press column in which I might write about anything—rather in the manner of, for example, Montale, although it was posthumously revealed that such a regularity was too much so that many of the pieces under his byline were ghosted. Well, there has never been much of a tradition of the like being offered a serious poet here so that was not going to happen. Imagine my surprise when our editor jumped and said yes. My weekly or monthly is down to termly but never mind, I shall not need a ghost.

Why haven't I settled for a blog? I don't know. I only know that I resist it. Perhaps I simply do not like the word. I can think only of a bog blah blah. I have a lot to say though I do not always know how to say it and if I appear, only appear, impertinent enough to compare my little writings to Saramago's it becomes clear that I hardly know how to bring myself to say very much. It is then with admiration, and inspiration, that I read these celebrations and castigations of matters close to home and worldly by an extraordinary novelist. Saramago's subjects take in literary and non-literary friendships, Bush, Obama, Berlusconi, social and political and financial hope and injustice and corruption, the real and the ridiculous—things British get a couple of glancing blows—and, what especially concerns me for the moment, the Palestinian and Israel, to which he returns time and again. It puts me to shame that I omitted two poems in particular from my 2005 selected *Miscanthus* that were included in my 1987 collected *The Resting Bell.*

Do
People change—
Or Israel
what can I do
or refuse you
as easily as I do
my birth.

*

Here
O Israel
you are doing it here.
For all
pass over your rights
for all pass over
your safe conducts.
There is no doubt
you are quite
human
and henceforth
like anyone
else.

The Face of Fernando Pessoa

An entry in *The Notebook* "On the Impossibility of Such a Portrait", in which Saramago revisits a foreword he wrote to an exhibition catalogue of portraits of the multi-faceted poet reminds me that Pessoa *has another portrait* and therefore another heteronym of which I don't think he himself ever dreamt. In July 2008, two months before Saramago began his blog, I met up in Portugal with Prof. T from Tokyo who was there to deliver a paper on Irish literature. Strolling past a souvenir shop one of her delegate colleagues—from the Netherlands, if I remember correctly—spoke up: Look, they are selling mugs with a picture of James Joyce. Knowing that Durban, where Pessoa spent many early years, is not Dublin, it fell upon me, ungraciously perhaps, to disabuse the group of the idea that the whole of Oporto was celebrating the presence of an academic conference. No, I said, that's a likeness of the great Portuguese poet Fernando Pessoa. Was I mistaken? A few days later—no, it was earlier—T and I had visited Lisbon where we sat conversing with an exceptionally bronzed Pessoa at a table set before a favourite café A Brasileira. It didn't occur to me then to ask him.

Allow me a last conceit about Saramago. As I write I have in front of me a little letter signed José Saramago, Lanzarote, May 10, 2000. I had sent him, in the care of his publisher, my little book with a story "On the 31st July" in which the British Isles improves itself by irreversibly standing on its head during the course of a solar eclipse—it must have happened, at least I wish it had happened, because there is a satellite photo on the back of the cover to prove it. The narrator refers to two precedent geographical irregularities, one of them Saramago's *The Stone Raft* in which the Iberian peninsular breaks off from the Rest of Europe, in this event not without certain catastrophic consequences though restorative in the end. I feel honoured to have received the courtesy of Saramago's thank you—from an island in the Atlantic.

I had thought too to write about Saramago's delightful memoir *Small Memories* but I am already over my word limit. That may be reason enough to begin a blog baa baa but an explanation for my wariness has just occurred to me. In the wrong hands, with no editor or other moderating influence to say Enough, the web's potential for democracy easily turns to dictatorship, even if only of one.

NOTE

José Saramago, *The Notebook*, trans. Amanda Hopkinson and Daniel Hahn (London & New York, Verso, 2010). The two "Israel" poems were first printed in Anthony Barnett, *North North, I Said, No, Wait a Minute, South, Oh, I Don't Know (148 Political Poems)* (Lewes, privately printed, 1985), reprinted in *The Resting Bell* (Lewes, Allardyce, Barnett, 1987); the book that does not reprint them is *Miscanthus: Selected and New Poems* (Exeter, Shearsman, 2005). "On the 31st of July" is included in *Lisa Lisa: Two Prosays* (Lewes, Allardyce Book, 2000), the precedent geographical irregularities being Cees Nooteboom's *In the Dutch Mountains* (English trans. 1987), in which the Pyrenees take themselves off to the Netherlands, or vice versa, and Saramago's *The Stone Raft* (English trans. 1994). There is a curious editorial error in *The Notebook* in footnoting the origin of Saramago's Pessoa foreword to the catalogue *Fernando Pessoa: A Galaxy of Poets, 1888–1935*, the title of a library and theatre foyer small exhibit presented by the London Borough of Camden in assoc. with the Portuguese Ministries of Foreign Affairs and Culture in October 1985, with a rather pedestrian foreword by José Blanco, chair of the exhibition committee. Saramago's imaginative foreword appeared in the catalogue to a different, substantial, exhibition, *Um Rosto para Fernando Pessoa: obras de trinta e cinco artistas portugueses contemporâneos* (Lisboa, Centro de Arte Moderna da Fundação Calouste Gulbenkian, 1985), which is referenced in the former. And, no, much as one might wish to entertain the idea José Blanco is not a pen name for Saramago. Saramago's *Small Memories* (English trans. 2009) encapsulates a childhood.

The review referred to in paragraph two considered some books about George Oppen. It appeared in *The Use of English*, vol. 60, no. 2 (spring 2009).

Ai Weiwei's Blog

Just when *A & O* is ready for press a selection from a remarkable more-than-daily blog of equally human proportions from the other side of the world, tempered with what on this side of the world is impassioned and deadpan ironies, also makes it to print: *Ai Weiwei's*

Blog: Writings, Interviews, and Digital Rants, 2006–2009, ed. & trans. Lee Ambrozy, & others (Cambridge, MA, & London, WritingArt Series, MIT Press, 2011): "The whole city is like a poorly assembled and cheap stage where all the people passing through it—men, women, the young, and the old—were nothing more than props, all part of an unsightly performance on culture, history, and political achievements."—from the entry "Different Worlds, Different Dreams", trans. Eric Abrahamsen. "It is the same under any dynasty: there are too many people here with ordinary trifles, sharing their pains and joys. One thing remains constant: these pains and joys are all fragmentary, they cannot be truly described or expressed, they cannot be multiplied or rendered, they can only be sensed, they are unutterable."—from the entry "Hypnosis and Fragmented Reality: Li Songsong", trans. Philip Tinari. In fact, there are many pages from which one might wish to quote. On the damage done to Tibet: "I will never visit that place, even if there were increasingly modern means of transportation. There is no reason, and no need to go. I want to learn how to maintain the distance between us."—from the entry "A Road with No End". Originally, Ai was invited, obliged almost, to blog by the authorities, those same authorities who closed him down in 2009. The blog is well read alongside *Ai Weiwei Speaks*, with Hans Ulrich Obrist (London, Penguin, 2011). A confession: I visited Ai's 100 million hand-painted ceramic sunflower seeds in the Turbine Hall at Tate Modern in 2010. I stole a handful, two handfuls in fact, in sight of a notice saying don't. My justification was an interview in which Ai said that if he were a visitor he would take one (he did not say a handful, or two handfuls, it is true) but I would have done it anyway. I began to give them away at Christmas in little boxes with a note that reads do not eat forever keep.

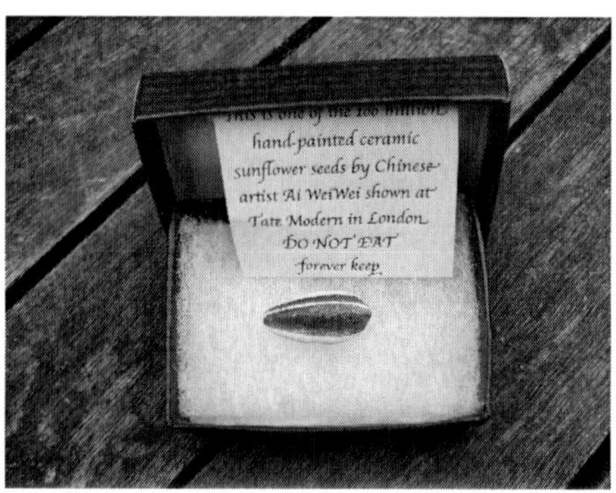

The Artist ['muŋk] Tries to Speak

Publication of a magnificent six-volume illustrated edition of *Vincent van Gogh: The Letters* (London, Thames & Hudson, 2009), brilliantly annotated and contextualized, reminds that the writings of another painter, also translated into English, have not fared so well.

The Story of Edvard Munch (London, Arcadia, 2001) by Norwegian novelist and romantic pianist Ketil Bjørnstad, the original published in 1993, fictionalizes in 386 monstrous pages the artist's life through an injudicious extracting from the letters and notebooks, his own and his contemporaries', interspersed with recast press reports and the author's clod-hopping present-tense interference. In Torbjørn Støverud and Hal Sutcliffe it has better translators than it deserves. The supposed reality (I suppose) of the narrating does nothing to dispel the myths, which are in dire need of being dispelled. Why, why, why, cannot Munch be left to speak for himself? All that is needed, all that is wanted, is the mass of Munch's own writings. Annotated, yes. Messed with, no.

Very few artists have left such a legacy of literacy so it is better to settle for Poul Erik Tøjner's *Munch: In His Own Words* (Munich, Berlin, London, New York, Prestel, English ed., 2003 [the original 2001, it would appear]). At least this delightfully presented largish format book places the selections from Munch's writings in sensible and relevant contexts, among photos and colour reproductions. Tøjner's at times overstressed, at times naïve, commentary is easily forgiven because of his perceptions: "There is one constant element that is more significant than all others in Munch's work and that is the glance—the eye. If one wants to see people looking, one need go no further than the work of Munch. Few other painters have painted the eye, painted sight, painted the glance, painted the gaze, or the look, to the same degree." The facing page reproduction of *Portrait of the Artist's Sister Inger* illustrates, in its full-frontal intensity, one aspect of Tøjner's observation.

So, it was with eager anticipation that, while preparing this piece, I chanced upon what I did not know: *The Private Journals of Edvard Munch: We Are*

Flames Which Pour Out of the Earth (Madison, University of Wisconsin Press, 2005). Here, surely, I would find a substantial presentation of Munch's writings, even if doubtless again just a selection of them, left to speak for themselves. I needn't have bothered and, I suppose (that suppose again), I might have been forewarned by the choice of an only seemingly appropriate quotation for the subtitle. The book is a scrappy editing job—and this despite the, as so often, fulsome grant and other assistance acknowledgements—though, I have no reason to doubt, otherwise more or less adequately translated. "Left to speak for themselves", I wrote a moment ago. I should say so, though not quite in the way I was envisioning.

"I have not tried to follow any chronological order in organizing the sections", editor and translator J. Gill Holland writes. But there are no delineated sections unless a few black and white plates of lithographs and drypoints somewhere over halfway through are supposed to divide things in two. I don't think so. What the editor presents are sequentially numbered texts, all of which look like poems. Except that many of them are nothing to do with poems or any other kind of imaginative writing but are, for example, concerned with the everyday, and the numbering bears no relation to anything in Munch or the Munch archive. There is no context, no annotation, only a generalized discursive introduction. The reader new to these, by turns reasoned and impassioned, writings will find no indication whether the poem-look is Munch's—deliberate or simply tracking the shape of the space available on the page on which he wrote—or the editor's interpretation or intervention. The game is given away by Frank Høifødt's perfunctory foreword: "A complete and scholarly presentation belongs to the future." Why? Why the future? Why not now? Why not before now?

It is to Tøjner's work, not referenced by Holland, that one must turn for answers and insights through reproductions of some of the manuscripts, often in variously coloured paints and crayons and childlike caps. The typography, here in Jennifer Lloyd's translation, mostly respects the uppercase of the painterly poems and imaginings as opposed to the more normal writing of the prosaic journal entries, quotidian, verging on the philosophical, contemplating painting and loving and journeys abroad. There are inconsistencies in this presentation but where there are I can see why and doubtless they were a designer's choice.

Valuable literature of one sort or another is to be found among only a handful of painters close to our times. Van Gogh for one. Munch for another. The new edition, however welcomed, of Van Gogh's writings is the latest of several. But of Munch's, until that long overdue "complete and scholarly presentation", or simply a trustworthy reading edition, materializes, we continue to have, both in the original and in translation, only a glimpse and if one picks up the wrong book a befuddled one at that.

THE TREE OF KNOWLEDGE

FOR

BETTER OR FOR WORSE

Letter to a Photographer

"Jack isn't making himself clear. If these duties were not imposed on us by the masters, it's obvious that we should not strive to perform them well in the masters' presence and badly in their absence. We should just perform them!" is a passage from Louis-René Des Forêts' story "The Children's Room", in which an apparent auditory voyeur, ear to the door—an eavesdropper though voyeur seems a much more appropriate word—listens to a group of children quasi-philosophically discussing and acting out a scenario of idiotic school rules. He says apparent because by the end of the story, at the end, the overhearer is revealed not to be the immoralist the reader has been led to believe. He will not give the game away.

For many months he has been engaged in translating Louis-René Des Forêts' *Poèmes de Samuel Wood*, a meditation on life and language and loss, the loss of others who are loved as well as of the self. And now this task he has set himself, for whatever unclear reason, unless it is clear, is almost done.

In the hope of gaining some last minute insight into the work, which might improve though not perfect his translation, he has turned to reading some other works by Des Forêts. (He pauses here to reflect on a group of excitedly chattering children in uniform, composed mainly but not entirely of girls, just passing the café window table at which he is sitting writing. Oh, here comes another. There goes another.) Among them a volume he has owned for many years that collects a novel and some stories but that he had thought he had neglected by giving it only an occasional cursory glance, always to give up on it. But this is not true. As he begins to read he realizes he has already read it through and through. For example, the story "The Great Moments of a Singer" is set in London. He recognizes the dark cloud that descends upon him as the word appears on the page. A cloud that descended when last he read it because of the reality, or the bad dream, of that city in which he believes himself terribly hurt by the past. And there in the story "Disorderly Silence", set among the tyranny of pupils and teachers, which perhaps has the salutary effect of giving him to understand that he has never really been alone in such experiences, is the visible mark of his previous reading, his writing in the margin wondering about the translation of a particular word. (It doesn't matter which.)

Dear Sh, he writes (which may be her name or shy or hush): I know that you have told me that it is time to stop writing and to draw.

Can it be that she who knows beautifully how to take a photograph and make a drawing (though he has yet to see more than one such drawing in a little notebook) beyond and before the taking and the making of mere gestures, though she says it is difficult, can possibly hold in esteem his little things, which is all he can call them? Or is he being teased? Or is he being bashful? Or neither or both? But he knows it cannot be true that he is an artist because writing comes to him only with difficulty, whereas these little squiggles of his come easily, so long as he always sticks to the first attempt. If he tries to redo them they never work. So he is a writer. He has to write. He has to do what is difficult. Even if he cannot write at all. And here is a conundrum, a double bind: if he does not write, when he cannot write, because he is lazy, which sometimes he certainly is, or because of some more substantial cause, his predisposition to anxiety increases. Yet, when he is writing, when he can write, he is wracked with guilt, unless wracked be too strong a word, because that is not what was supposed to be in store for him, though the very early insistence of others that he should read and read must have given him a head start. A regret?

How impatient he is to finish this now, he who pretends (does he really pretend?) to believe an old saw (he has repeated it so often) of intellectual strength and emotional vulnerability. He refuses the more honest word weakness. Quite the coward.

He has made a drawing to accompany his translation of Louis-René Des Forêts' *Poèmes de Samuel Wood*. It is supposed to be a tree. But looking at it now he sees that it is also an uncanny likeness of its author—or perhaps Samuel Wood. He finds this extraordinary and mysterious. For a moment he allows himself to escape writing and to be the artist she would like him to be.

NOTE

The Children's Room (Calder, 1963), Jean Stewart's translation renders Jacques as Jim; here he is reinstated as Jack; *Poèmes de Samuel Wood* (Fata Morgana, 1988); *Poems of Samuel Wood*, with the drawing (Allardyce Book, 2011).

The Publisher

It was very kind of her to invite me to one of her salon evenings. I was very glad I said no, graciously at first, later intemperately. I have only myself to blame for unwittingly setting the whole thing up because I contacted her in the first place with a forthright comment, I couched it politely, about something to do with one of her good authors, though the comment was about something not so good, about an English *critic*, *anthologizer*, *memoirist*, in fact a *mediocrity*, whose misdemeanours included offences against myself and my erstwhile colleagues, with whom she had put her interesting German author in conversation, at one of her salon evenings. She responded with what I did think was suspiciously unjustified enthusiasm and generosity, I was momentarily taken in, because I wanted to be, I am now confirmed in interpreting first and foremost her desire to cultivate a literary contact who might turn out to be useful. Well, she didn't know me, did she, so she should have been more circumspect before deciding to think of someone such as myself as an opportunity. Somewhere in the back of my mind, if not further forward, I expect, though to be honest, I agree, I saw her like that too. Nevertheless, she did say she would like to see a poem or two, as if I could agree to make such a miniscule pick from what I wrote in clusters, racemes, chords, not to be pulled apart too severely, so to speak. How was she to understand why I would not attend her soiree at which one of *those* poets would be reading, or even if one of *these* poets were to be. How was she to know. Siren at the fountain. How could I possibly explain why to one so intent on entertaining the worst of that band of editors and scribblers, that circus of a cabal, though there is nothing much secret about it, going round and around rewarding each member in turn with a poison, a prize, a review, a publication. So I packaged up some books and took them to the post office. I thought at least some of the translations might be of interest to her, right up her metropolis street, I thought. You see, I am living in what seems to be a cross between The Fairy Tale Town and The Little Town Where Time Stood Still. I haven't heard a thing. And I must remember not to make my writing too small, I keep telling myself, or lean too far out of a window for that matter.

A few hours after deciding this must be the finish a message arrived *I am impressed.* (But where to put the emphasis . . .) If I fail to add this I shall be doing her a disservice, leaving the impression she must indeed have taken umbrage, she was perfectly entitled to, though it does no justice to a satisfactory ending.

I haven't heard anything else, oh yes, press releases.

NOTE

"The Fairy Tale Town" is the title of a story by Robert Walser, who wrote in a microscript; *The Little Town Where Time Stood Still* is the title of a novel by Bohumil Hrabal, who leant too far out. Other literary references are anybody's guess—not anyone's, anybody's.

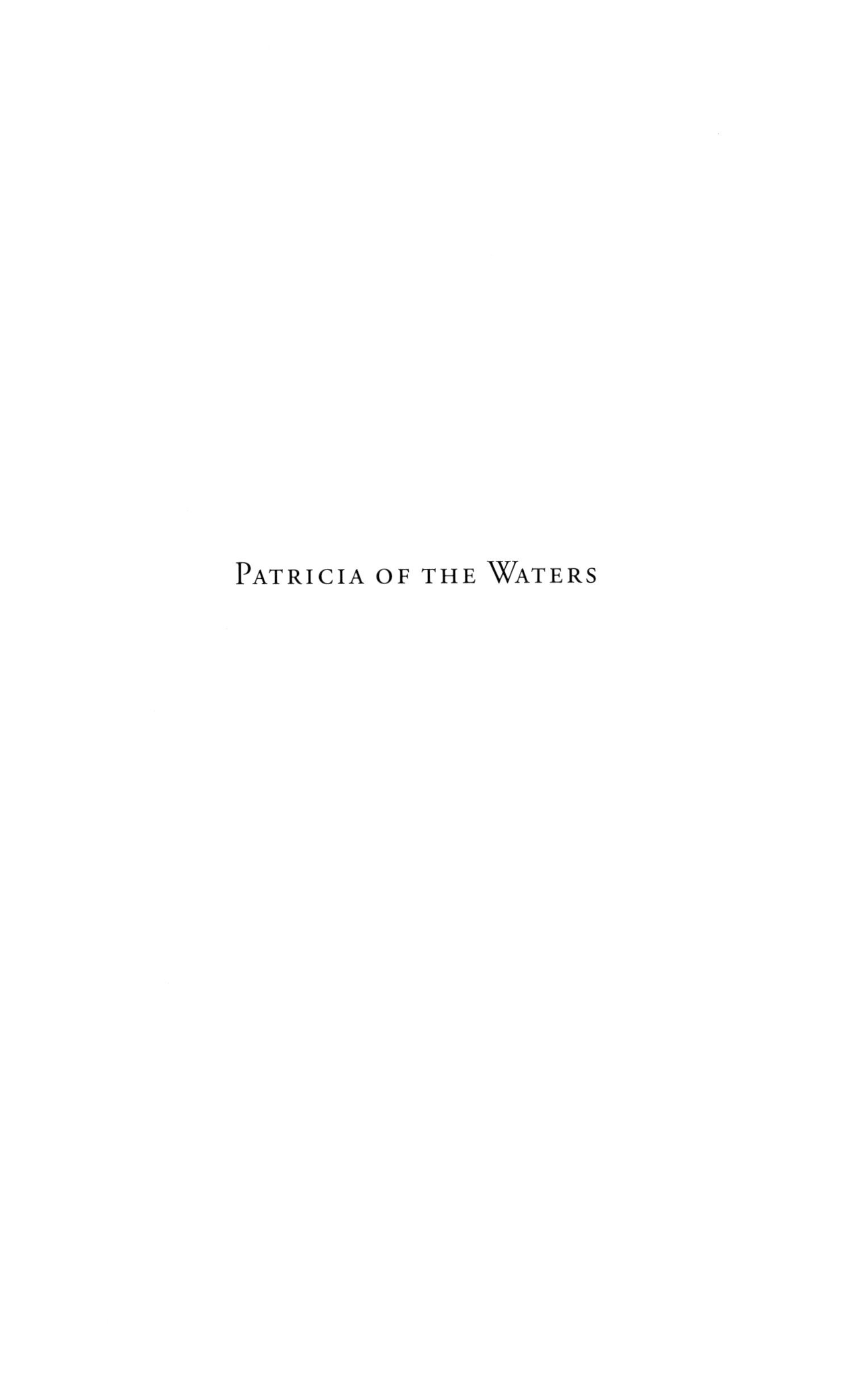

Patricia of the Waters

Patricia of the Waters

What shall I write about Patrizia Dell'Acqua of Berlin? In the photograph of her face, her half face, I should better say, which I received in the mail from her today, Friday the thirteenth, postmarked the day of the eclipse (I am no cabbalist nor superstitious) the clenched knuckles of her left hand, forming a V with her slender long-nailed thumb, have drawn the collar of what appears to be a shiny black leather jacket up over her mouth, covering the whole of the lower part of her face below her nostrils and her left earring. Centred are her beautiful mysterious brown eyes, or so they appear. Her black straight hair, full yet slightly boyish, parted on the left, is clipped at the top edge. This is the second photograph of Patrizia Dell'Acqua she has given me. More than seventeen years ago, when she was just eighteen, with the intellect and bearing of a woman in her twenties, she sent a photograph of herself at sixteen, I believe, in which she wore a long dress. I no longer have it. I tore it up and threw it out in order to forget her when I understood that she would not be returning from Berlin after Christmas. Now the pupils of her eyes in their almond setting focus once again on the beholder, her first male lover, recipient and spectator, but also beyond him, if I am not mistaken, within her.

*

Is it right that I should write about Patrizia? Is it right for her? Is it right for me? She has read the opening passage and it meets with her approval. At least that is what she says and I assume that she believes it as well as means it. In answer to my question she says that she has no objection to my writing about what has happened to her, about what she has told me and about what I imagine. Her two conditions are that I use her name and that I let her read what I have written before it is published.

*

When the faceless becomes known such as the assassin or the terrorist on camera.

*

—Patrizia, you are wrong. I have never denied the historicity of my Jewish ancestry, its culture, a legendary and mythological status if you like. But I deny the religion as I would any other. Which does not mean that I do not believe in a higher order (nor does it mean that I do). —But how do you separate them? —I can't explain. I haven't worked that out. I just feel it. —Is it because you were not taught to be religious? . . . I know that you think I must be nuts. Wanting to read Rabbinical studies. . . . —It's not that . . . I just uttered a forbidden word. There's no such word as can't according to my father. . . . And to feel provoked wrath. Not the anger of the moment at I don't feel like doing the washing up. But outrage that a momentous decision might be determined by feelings. As if they did not exist, or if they did, as if their existence were a personal affront. There, Patrizia, the comma after exist instead of or places it firmly in the emotions not the intellect. —It would if it were not the intellect opting for the emotion.

*

For every one thing one says there is another one or more things to say. Opposite or to the side.

*

—Do you still smoke? —I've never really smoked. I get through a packet of Gitanes a year. Maybe two. It's never been a problem for me. I can have a cigarette and not touch another for six months. Or I'll smoke every now and then for a week or so and then stop. If my writing is going well, for example. Like a French poet, except the French don't smoke Gitanes, they prefer British and American tobaccos. The tobacco is always smokier on the other side. I'm not a real smoker. I don't inhale. I just like the aroma of dark tobacco. Pipe and cigar smokers don't inhale so why should I. Why do you ask? Are you a smoker? —Don't you know? Of course I am. I haven't been able to stop. You smoked when I knew you. —What? —You told me I had a bad influence on you. —So I did. It's coming back. You remember that? —Everything. I remember everything.

*

Like the Romans, legions of books entered the English language from abroad only to go out of print leaving little trace that they were ever here. True or false. The legions weren't so many and they found the going tough.

*

Protestantism is the legacy of barbarism. But not the only one.

*

Patrizia's mother and stepfather are Berliners. Her Italian father, a Catholic from the South of the Country, died in her infancy. Her grandmother survived the war outside Berlin. A secret Jew.

*

I'm gullible. Not naïve. Gullible. If I ever write an autobiography its title will be Gullible's Troubles.

*

I don't always know whether to believe everything Patrizia tells me. Sometimes it seems as if she is trying too hard to make herself sound interesting. Too many anecdotes, of destiny. Unlikely or likely. Whether or not they are true they could just as easily be clichés. My doubts disappoint her. —I'm very angry that you don't believe me. —I do believe you. I apologize. People look askance when I relate some of my own experiences so I know what it's like and I should know better.

*

You take things personally that are the human condition because you are not forewarned.

*

The wrecking of Europe.

*

I began writing about Patrizia. But now I'm more intent on writing about myself or some grey area of macrocosmic aphoristic philosophy between us for which I am ill equipped. As usual I am unable to hold together a narrative thread. It's not my forte. So why do I feel I ought to be able to do it? Or that it's necessary? I should do what I can and be happy. But that's not work, is it? Doing what you are capable of doing or enjoy doing.

*

You don't have to be Jewish to feel guilty but it helps. Catholic too.

*

—These fragmentary stabs say something about the condition of our existences. —Ours? Do you mean yours and mine? Or everybody's? —Let's keep this between ourselves. —Our own bodies. —Our elves.

*

Avoidance. Avoidance of the difficult task. Evasion. Evasion of the story-telling. But not the truth-telling. Be careful. L. (R.) J. is not a role model. Too clinical an oddity. Is Patrizia a pretext? Though more than no more than one?

*

Today's newspaper, I've returned from reading *The Times* (let's set that in *The Times*—or even *The Times* New Roman so that you can see what dreadful bookfaces they make) in a café because I don't want the damn' things in the house, reports new research showing that size does matter, cf. Renault's Clio ad. Women seek out tall men. Those taller than the survey's average 5ft 7 are more likely to find a mate and father children, the taller the more. At 5ft 7½—still?—I'm not sure where I stand. Let's convert that to 171.45 cm. Would I do better in Sicily, or Cornwall, where the men are short, than in Norway, where the men are tall? I didn't do too badly. Whatever went wrong must have been my fault. Or no fault at all.

*

The same newspaper reports on the progress of the libel action brought by a Holocaust denying historian against an academic and her publisher. I wonder whether he's read Primo Levi?

*

Why don't philosophers take on great poets? Fear? Contempt? There aren't that many poets worth taking on. Or philosophers. But that's not the reason. Zanzotto is a great poet. Césaire. Vallejo. I want to read Eco on Zanzotto. Every great poem knocks into a cocked hat the latest literary theory. But the theorists don't want to hear that. When they're not writing about themselves French literary philosophers (sometimes) write about poets. English literary philosophers (only) write about French literary philosophers. Obviously this is true (only) up to a point.

*

I understand why Primo Levi rejected Celan's complexities. But I understand Celan too. As far as I am able. One fell in the water the other to the floor.

*

—No. Patrizia. I cannot go to Israel. It's out of the question. (It always has been.) You know that I was invited to spend the Millennium in Norway in the mountains. As much as I wanted to go for one reason or another I decided not to. I wanted to be there but not to get there. I invited you here. How could I meet you in Israel?

*

Everyone should know by now that the English millennium has two ns. It's taken a while.

*

Patrizia kisses me down the telephone. —Oh. —I think my sexuality is pathological. —Why do you think that? Because you were violated? —Yes, I think so. I started suffering eating disorders. Probably because I didn't tell anyone.

*

—What am I doing? Writing about you like this. I shouldn't be telling you what I'm doing. I'm afraid I'm using you. Absolving myself from obligation by telling you. Why do you let yourself be used? —No. It's all right. You can write whatever you like. . . . Don't tell me what you write. Not now. . . . —Are you using me, too?

*

—We're both losing sight of things. You know we can only be friends. Intellectually. Intimately if circumstances allow and that's what we want. Nothing more. Anything else would spell disaster. It's too much of a risk, already. . . . The love she professes sounds destructive. It would even at the best of times. She talks of symbiosis. Two becoming one so that one thinks one cannot live without the other. She says love is that. I know all about that. I don't know whether to take what she says seriously or not. Fantasay.

*

After half-a-life-time, half of that working wherever I am living in my own time at my own pace, I still break out in sweat at the thought of having to get up and travel in grey to an office in the City or anywhere. Or those wasted afternoons as a flâneur in white (flannels) waiting in the outfield for a ball that never comes only to miss it when it does.

*

Patrizia carries the various parts of her worlds on her shoulders. A sickness unto death. Her decision to visit London like this is irrational. Intuition. She scares the life out of me. She's imposing her will. I didn't invite her to spend a few days over the December–January cusp in my little provincial town an hour's train journey away from the capital for that. She's overstepped the mark. Leaving a disquieting message on my answerphone. No discussion because I wasn't awake to pick the receiver up. Ringing so early so eager to buy the ticket three months in advance. My cooling off, below zero, angers her. In this matter she has no appreciation of negotiation. It was a bad idea. I should have known better. I'm to be held responsible if she transfers, and changes, her course of studies from Berlin to London. —London won't make you happy. —My psychiatrist says I should settle down and finish my studies. —She's right! If you have the capacity to settle down. First it's medicine, then it's biochemistry, then it's clinical psychology, then it's rabbinical studies, and all the while it's English and literature and English. All these subjects running around in your head like headless chickens. Should you be studying at all? Can you focus on one subject to completion. I'm not sure that you can. Shouldn't you just write, that's what's important to you? —I don't feel complete without finishing a degree. —I can understand that. I felt like that. —It'll take about five years in Berlin. I can probably do it in two or three in England. I think it's easier. —Maybe it is. I don't know anything about the system in Germany. —I have to study with all these people who know less than me. I know more than the teachers but there are no concessions. —I don't have an answer for you.

*

Walter Benjamin cracked. Spectacles. Das Passagen- should not be put into Arcades. It lacks the ambiguous clarity of the only one of his galleries in which it exists.

*

I am so unaccustomed to being paid for what I do that if I sell a copy of one of my books I feel I must be ripping someone off. That's why I'm always giving them away.

*

—I didn't use contraception those months we were together. —I'd ask you if it was all right and you'd nod in the affirmative. —We might have had a child. —You'd still have gone away. You'd have found a woman. —No, I'd have stayed. —I don't think so, Patrizia, don't you remember asking me to give you a child so that you could bring it up alone? You were always falling in love with women. —Older women. —That's what you told me. —I find women beautiful. —I find them beautiful too. —If it had happened I might have stayed. —I'd like to believe you but I don't. —We amused ourselves in the town looking at the young women, choosing one we'd both enjoy, who would let us. —We might have done something about it. —Half-heartedly.

*

The intrigue of photos, paintings too, that show streets, landscapes too, as they once were, seen alongside shots as they are now.

*

Fascinating the way books read in the bath get wet so the pages buckle with an ancient parchment-like quality. I'd like to wet a whole print run of booklets to sell like that.

*

The narrative escapes again.

*

"Another time I had accidentally written such a good dictation that the French teacher accused me of copying and refused to believe my denials."

—Valéry Larbaud, "Rose Lourdin", *Enfantines*. I recall a shaming, more than shameful, incident. When I was nine or so. Our teacher, to whom I looked up, I might have been in love, set us to write a story. Originality eluded me. I stole a bubble-picture adventure, what the French call a bande dessinée, I think it took place in a cave, from the back, I'm sure it was the last page, or the penultimate page, of *Eagle*, the only comic, a superior one, allowed at home. A few days later, beautiful mistress of twenty-seven boys, or however many we were, she singled out the excellence of my story to be read in front of the class. Did I think I would get away with it? Though the words were mine the plot was not. Some fellow pupil piped up. My denials elicited her look of disdain. Difficult at such an age to say Yes, I have rewritten it. I returned I was returned to my desk. Thirty-five years later I taught a prep boarding class of privileged kids. Diplomats' daughters. Army officers' sons. Vice versa. I managed to get a not very bright but perfectly happy eleven year old apple grower's son to compose his first story. Just a paragraph. For him an achievement. "He got that from . . ." some TV animation, a boy's voice piped up. Pip squeak. Don't let his apple cheeks grow rosier. "I don't mind where he got the idea from so long as he's put it into his words." Who was I to humiliate a classmate who bore the stigma, stamen, of being christened Laxton? Laxton's Advance. Laxton's Fortune. Laxton's Reward.

*

At that time Patrizia lived with me in the tied farm cottage. —Let the school make use of your talent. I'm sure they'd pay you a little. She teaches the girls gymnastics an hour twice a week. Somersaults. Cartwheels. Vaults. Voluntarily. Nothing competitive. All smiles. Legs flying. Akimbo. Almost graceful. Boys too if they wish. But mostly the girls like that. Typically, like the fate that befalls those little East Europeans, Patrizia suffers her once supple championship adolescence with a racked back no coach ever led her to expect. The abuse in pursuit of the physical.

*

Man-child, man-child, look at the state you're in, as Neneh Cherry sings.

*

I have taken to reading novels in which paintings figure. The previous one by Torgny Lindgren, *Till Sanningens Lov,* although To Tell the Truth I think In the Name of Truth might be a better title than In Praise of Truth, the account of a picture-framer caught up in an historical forgery. An impresario grooms the picture-framer's childhood friend to be the biggest name in pop in Sweden, which happens to be the home of Neneh Cherry—although she isn't a forgery as the singer in the novel is—with whose stepfather I had the good fortune to play music. Sad to say a recording of the most memorable of those few occasions was wiped, or so I'm told, by a so-called flautist at The Royal Conservatory of Music in Copenhagen, where the concert took place, who had no sympathy for the kind of music we played. At the moment I am reading *Manual de Pintura e Caligrifa* by José Saramago, in English of course.

*

Patrizia's thirty-sixth birthday. —Can't you come to Berlin next week? You'll be in Paris and Geneva? —I can't come to Berlin. One day, perhaps. Not now. —I have to see you urgently. —Why? What's wrong? —I can't say. Not over the telephone. —Tell me. —My gynaecologist told me today that if I want to have a child I have to do something about it soon. According to the analysis. —You know it's a bad idea for us to have a child together. —Why? —You know why. We've talked about this. You've said it yourself. —Because I've been ill. —I thought you saw your pyschiatrist today? —No, yesterday. —Oh yes, we were talking about your birthday. —What if a child would help me be well? —That's no responsibility to place on either a child or a father. If you were steady it would be another matter. —You don't trust me and you're too scarred. —You understand perfectly. —Scared and scarred.

*

Caught. Patrizia has told an untruth I cannot call it a lie that casts doubt on other matters. I felt uneasy. I couldn't put my finger on it. It dawned on me when I awoke this morning. She could not have had tea with Lemon during her affair did she have one with Gianna Nannini. Lemon was dead before Patrizia and I ever met. Before their affair. Why has she felt compelled to match the photos and documents of my own crossing with Lemono? Yeah. Where was she?

*

Now I really do not know whether I am writing a fiction or not. My fiction? My reality? Patrizia's fiction? Patrizia's reality? Her multiple personalities? Or those of the book? As long as they are not mine.

*

Patrizia has telephoned this evening from hospital. She does not expect to be well enough to visit London at the end of this month. I had not written anything to speak of for several weeks.

* * *

The book's changing. It leaves Patrizia behind, at least for the moment. At the same time it doesn't. I have to pick up the threads. Let's see if I can get down to work again.

* * *

It is years later. And I find myself visiting Berlin for the first time every now and then for reasons that are unrelated to Patrizia. I never heard from her again although I wrote her three maybe four times. I could have done more to try to find her. Perhaps I still can though I am not sure what. I have pangs of guilt, which does not make sense. I have pangs of guilt that do not make sense. Shall we pass each other in the street? I fear the worst. I have decided to publish this without her having read the rest of it.

* * *

*

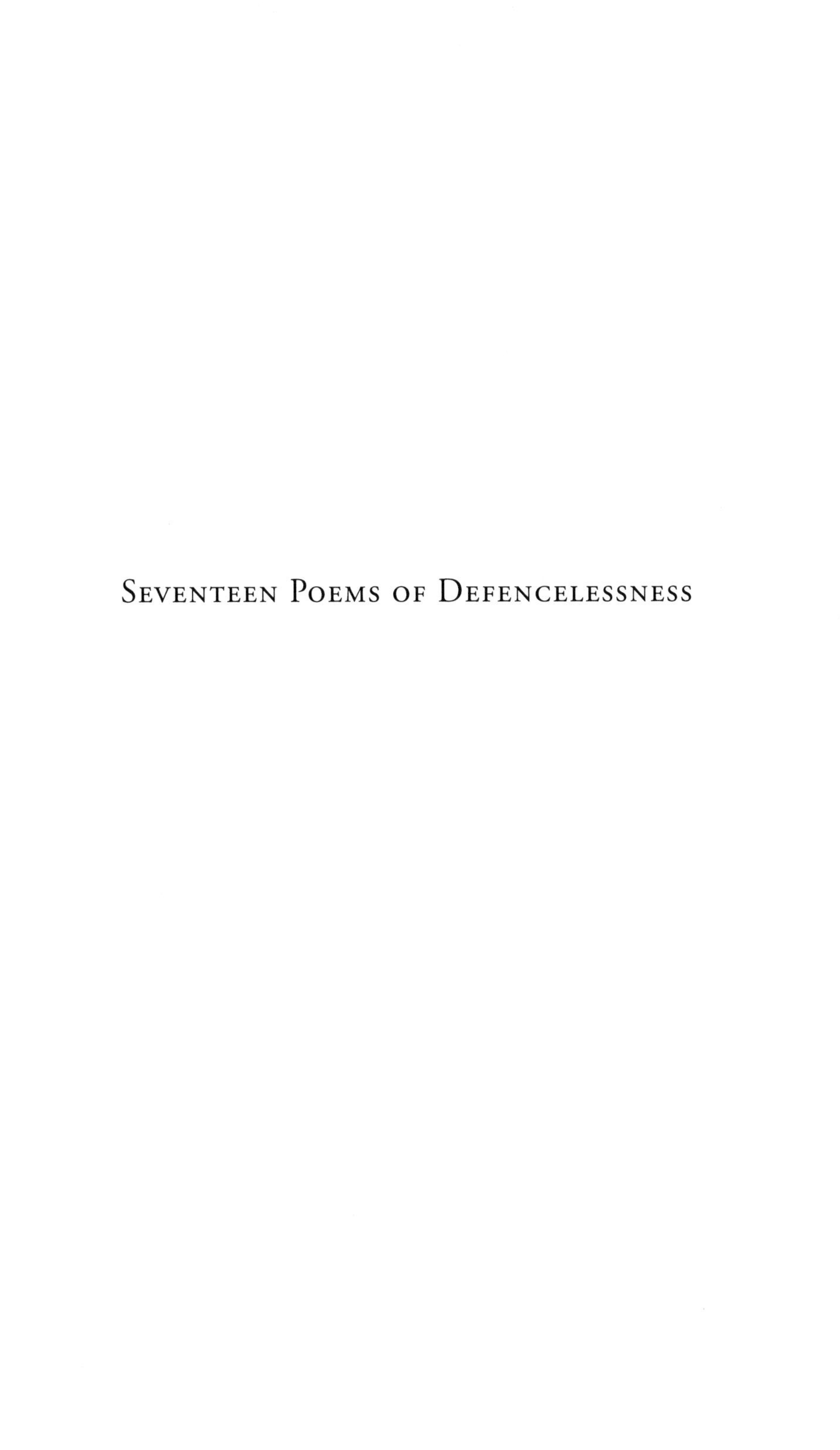

Seventeen Poems of Defencelessness

Arbitrariness

The art of simplicity
is not the art of the simple.
If it were it might be
that I had very little to say
assuming that already
not to be the case.

I have removed the jacket of your book
because I do not particularly want whoever
might be looking over our shoulders
in one of the many cafés we frequent
to catch even a glimpse of your
arrogance. Mine is enough.

Nevertheless, I have opened you
as a necessary antidote
to what is in danger of engendering
bitterness, if it has not already done
so. Bittersweet is alright.

Dishonest Poem

My memory is a slut.
I know exactly who I am.
Now that this is a closed book
I am calm.

Dissolved

This is the night the town in which I live—
I hesitate to say it is my town—
thinks it comes to life after the preparations
of the year.

For those who do not think about these things as I do—
and that goes for most—
this may be true.

However much it may rain—tonight
it is forecast—may not determine
whether or not the night turns out
to be a damp squib.

Or whether this tawdry pretence
at historical remembrance
may one day dissolve dissolve dis
sembled in the coldest of nights.

Fool

Is that a ring of betrothal on the fourth finger—
counting the thumb—of your left hand?
It is hard to tell because the hand for the ring
differs from culture to culture and I do not know
which culture is yours. Shall I risk making a fool
of myself whether it is or is not? Well, since
I am already a fool the risk is negligible.

Remembrance

It is with dismay that I think about writing another poem
along these lines. My imperious whore, my visited muse.
I suffer vertigo and nausea in a labyrinth of cleansed dirt.

Forget to Talk

I forget to talk about what I thought would be a sticking point
whether the emblem on your shoulder blade
is permanent or a transferral of feral instincts.

And here⌒I go against my word.

They make

They make such a song and dance.

Things I did
I should not have done
and other taunts.

Those terrible nostalgic words
"too late"

I'll go out in the snow

I'll go out in the snow, which has just begun to fall. It won't last long, at least not today
Flashes of light
To achieve this
They are starting now, if they have not already finished
It evades and avoids me
I sit down to write a story. As usual, nothing, to be truthful, very little. How I do understand *Blank* [1]
As if a single word is a whole book
And to delve further into the future, that little off-putting squint, a grimace in the work, definitely a grimace
They look very funny while they are eating
Intruding and extruding
She is said. Go to him

[1] *Blank* is a notebook by Roger Giroux

I elevated her in the dream

I elevated her in the dream, no, that's not right,
in the dream she was elevated from waitress to violinist,
this is very confusing, at least two appear to become one,
I am reticent to say have, I am not happy about this,
others in this other restaurant sit at too close tables,
their voices are-are interfering with what I want to say, it is
my fault, I arrived at a bad moment, abandoned

with love to you both

Far Off

Far off yet never so far
by the snow
a beautiful
anxiety
such a beautiful
face and ponytail
has my eye caught
the form the shape
each beauty
would be this face
observant
must be
slob slob slobber blubber
vertiginous vertigo

moon gestures
falling
frenetically distracted
hi yr phonetic
anxiety
tired
crystals
not icing
captive

Now It Is You I Pick Up

Now it is you I pick up.
I have left you untouched, except for a very occasional half-hearted dusting, for many many years.
Now that I reread you I do not know why it took so long. However, some of your lines have often resonated with me without, it seems, my always knowing it.

I receive a salutary lesson that reminds me of all I have almost forgotten. Wonderment. Astonishment. Joy. And other words that are no longer supposed to be used in certain circles.

Might I try to translate you again? But you have already been done to death. It was, then, not such a bad idea to keep you by me but not to pick you up.

I Have Never Written a Surrealist Poem in My Life

Let us remark upon the shirt without a collar
The typeface without a glyph
So tell me, tell me everything you know

That you are wretched
Despondent

I cannot find the word in the dictionary—
No wonder, you are spelling it incorrectly—

Do not go there
It is all Chinese

I cannot grasp what this is all about
It is not difficult to be tyrannical

Snowed under with the *News of* that *Warring Clan*

MANIFESTO

I am learning, though it is a slow job, that I must spell things out.

To leave things not exactly stated, which is not to say inexactly, for the one who reads, and that includes myself, to have to work out what mistakenly may go by the name ambiguity because it is not uncertainty that is invoked but multiple certainties that are is a mug's game.

What is more, I am caught between the foolishness of boring old conventions and the foolishness of experiments done in public, not made public, mind you, done in public.

O Mighty Caesar. O Mighty Caesar's wife.

PAGAN

Delightful.
Your delightful words.

In another part of this snowflake world
Threats do not stop and nothing will assuage
This dreadful pun.

His *is* off will not do.

The One

The one who blows up missed the point
or any other grammaticalization

Parisian Walk Out

To play at every little piece of language
For the nonproliferation of non-escalation. Apology.

I am lost without papers. In fiction, faceless.
Stalking out in crocodile fashion, the two of you.
I know. I was there. In poetry, recipient.
Eying for another. Turning to speak.

I understood by not understanding.
By opening the window. By staying silent. By talking.

I Am Defeated

I cannot bring myself to do too much today
Just enough, perhaps

You miserable uptight creatures

Oh dear, how can I get out of this

Why does the calvary horse not stay and say I shall not fight this battle
Opposing horse and rider and mine shall live another day

It would not make much difference the heat seeking bullet
Is nothing new

I am defeated

Icing and Noticing

Icing and Noticing

The Snow will always start off like a blank page as it is now and was in the past, until it is trampled, as it is now. He knows this is far from an original observation and that it is likely to be found fault with. One might say he can sing only one song.

He has to understand that he will be, can be, the kind of writer he thinks he would like to be. That he will, can be, the kind of writer that he is. The sooner he comes to terms with this the better. Then he may become the kind of writer he thinks he would like to be.

For many years he has been reluctant to write in these notebooks that were a gift. He was not sure how the paper would take to the pen. Or how the pen would take to the paper. Now that he has begun he finds that he need not have worried. He must tell her this straightaway. And indeed he does.

How delightful it is for him to walk in the road because of the snow. Where there are only stationary vehicles with icicles. Why is it delightful for him to walk where it is not usually possible?

Soaking in the bath it is only with difficulty that he can stop thinking about all those traces in the world of things he would like forgotten. Double you double you double you. His poem he now decries, the event accurately or falsely reported, or reported solely from another point of view, is no longer hidden away in some obscure publication unlikely to be chanced upon or opened if it is, or lost in a closed file.

Again he finds the writing veering away from what he would like to do. How does he come to decide what and when to write? Is it even a decision he makes for himself?

He has managed to track down the last set of winter tyres just before the second fall arrives.

I remember a day that became dark and a letter home.

If he is not feeling anxiety he thinks something must be wrong, so accustomed to it he has become.

The wagtail gave a crumb of comfort in the school grounds.

Doing poetry a disservice by not aspiring to greatness, knowing that it cannot be reached, by aspiring to greatness, knowing that it can be reached. What is he talking about?

That he learnt to eat the grape pip, not to spit it out. Frosted.

Hiding. As if he got in the way of his self.

An infusion of dried limes.

Fear of movement for fear of disturbance.

You play with your little string orchestra and you think you play very fine.

Ruins in the distance.

FROM

And When I Sleep I Do Not Weep

FROM

And When I Sleep I Do Not Weep

Am I a happy person whose happiness has been conspired against so that I live in an almost permanent anticipation of unhappiness? Which is far removed from Pessoan pessimism (the word I think of when I hear his name however pleased I may be to read him). But Pessoa says he is not a pessimist. Just like Celan says: absolutely not hermetic. Flying in the face of squinting world views. Squinting in the bottom of flying worlds.

A Broken Nose

I used to have a bad dream that if my mouth was gagged by robbers and my hands tied behind my back in such a way that would make it too difficult for me to free myself in time I might suffocate because I would not be able to breathe properly through the nostril that had become obstructed when the nasal septum was not reset professionally after it was broken during a game of rugby. Efforts to explain calmly to the robbers that they risked an accidental death on their hands, followed by mute gesticulations, were to no avail.

Writing

Ironic—a surfeit of irony is the Kingdom's illness whereas a meagre portion of it is the States'—that I have agreed that thirty years of my writing should be included in an indiscriminate (some would say democratic) megalopolitan database of English Poetry now that I have decided I no longer wish to be identified as a poet (I have never felt comfortable with that except privately where it makes no difference and does not matter), even though I continue to write poems. What sane, let alone insane, poet would want to be associated with the reception given to what passes for the limits of poetry in the paltry imagination of the great and the good and those administrating minions who disgrace it? Always thus. To say nothing of one's fellow poets, who are divided and ruled. Is poetry become a dirty word? Among poets, Yes. Yet poetry is where I am at home, and away from home. Prose? Roger Giroux wrote in a posthumously published notebook: "A self-respecting 'writer' has the duty to write only love letters. All the rest is servility and scribbling." And "What do publishers and readers want? A thoroughly conformist originality . . ."

I think of poets who published almost nothing in their lifetime and wonder why I should be so troubled.

In the Train

In the train the chattering monologue of one woman to another who cannot get her own word in and doesn't try. Relentless monotony unrelieved by the disruptive disrupted clatter of the wheels of a carriage well past its useful life. I was reading without reading. Suddenly I understood why and looked up. That interminable voice. And now I feel like a Pessoa in disquiet. A monoabi—though if there is a difference it is to do with woman. The physicality of a loved woman, so that I am not mono—even in (playing with words) a state of monogamy (monogyny).

However, it is said (however it is said) that Pessoa may never have known a woman but I am not so sure. I would wish him to have known a woman. Some literal literary evidence suggests that he did not. Some does.

. . .

TO BE SERIOUS IN A WORLD THAT IS NOT SERIOUS

*

TO BE LIGHTHEARTED IN A WORLD THAT IS NOT LIGHTHEARTED

. . .

TRUE to myself in the varieties of my style, my stylus, my type of writing I am unfashionable yet never out of style, ever.

. . .

MY HEAD closed down shutting in my thinking. Just to tell a story would be a relief. To tell the truth? as I might begin.

What I want to put down struggles with what I am able to put down.

WHITE

"WHO gets no snow makes it himself:" I am truly dazzled by Nooteboom's notebook. I see nothing but blinding truth in it.

. . .

UNBELIEVABLE nervousness that a desired woman thinks I am desirable. That a beautiful woman says I am beautiful. So what is the matter? Nothing is the matter. To be desired as much as I desire. Believe it.

Dark : White

The characters in Tanizaki's fiction desire the perfection of a woman with milk white skin. Tanizaki himself *In Praise of Shadows* honours the secret flush, blush, glow of a dark skin.

. . .

A book too easily something for everybody must be a promiscuous book.

. . .

I shall be however many years old this year. But I feel it as little different as if it were sixteen or twenty-six.* Have I learnt anything? Have I come to anything? It is not quite the same thing to ask whether I have amounted to anything. Or accounted for anything. *With one exception: now and then an ache in the head, and on the right side of the forehead, at having seen too much argument.

. . .

When does fantasy become reality? When does it remain itself?

. . .

On the night of 24th to 25th October A had the following dream, more or less. He had the use of a largish complicated house in the countryside—in France? He was waiting somehow for Honesty, with whom there had sometimes been talk about making a baby. Then in some kind of bar or restaurant he was approached by ?, a character in an English TV soap opera who appeared to have a sapphic crush on another straight but vulnerable character. At the first meeting ? very quickly asked A to make her pregnant. Soon her father and mother came up and ? introduced them. Astonished and confused and wondering about his loyalty to Honesty he took ? to the house in the country, where they made love. Or fucked would be the more appropriate word. He fucked her in the dream. Mainly from behind with her rear rearing curving thrusting lasciviously up towards him. The scene changed back to the largish bar before his, ?their, orgasm(s). He stood at the bar with Honesty. ?'s father saw him from the far side of the room, smiled, and was about to come over but A looked at him, shook his head discreetly, and put his arm round Honesty. ?'s father quickly took stock of the situation, nodded, and stayed where he was. Wake up more or less.

. . .

He has a beard which is supposed to be dark but is now white, silver or grey according to how one views it, dark hair which is still dark and glasses which may or may not be dark because they change with the light.

. . .

The poet grows old but not old enough, not jaded, enough to leave his modernism behind.

. . .

Guo xiaolu is a writer. She is a writer. One of her stories is entitled "The Mountain Keeper". Such a story makes me think of her as the one who watches over stories.

. . .

Love of evergreen (some evergreen) because less sense of loss. But the seasons, the seasons.

* * *
*

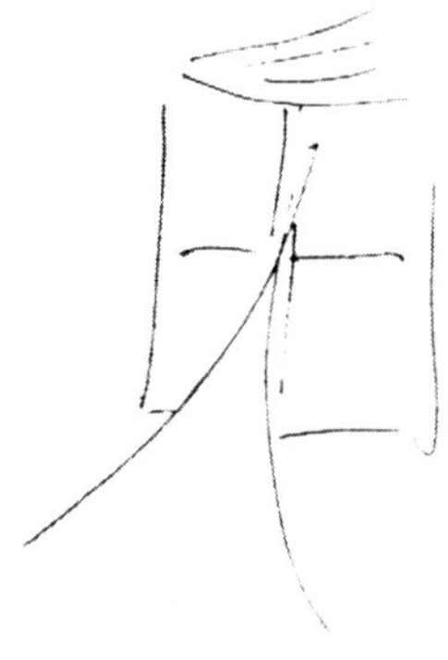

Two drawings

Logic, for the frontispiece to Alain Delahaye, The Lost One (1989)

A–Z of Mountain Paths, for the cover of Poems by Andrea Zanzotto (1993)